PAMPHLETS ON AMERICAN WRITERS • NUMBER 38

UNIVERSITY OF MINNESOTA

✓ *Conrad Aiken*

BY REUEL DENNEY

UNIVERSITY OF MINNESOTA PRESS • MINNEAPOLIS

Printed in the United States of America at
the North Central Publishing Company, St. Paul

Library of Congress Catalog Card Number: 64-64445

Permission to use the excerpts from *Collected Poems* (published
by Oxford University Press, copyright 1953) and *Selected Poems*
(published by Oxford University Press, copyright 1961)
was granted by Conrad Aiken.

Distributed to high schools in the United States by Webster Division
McGraw-Hill Book Company, Inc.
St. Louis   New York   San Francisco   Dallas

PUBLISHED IN GREAT BRITAIN, INDIA, AND PAKISTAN BY THE OXFORD UNIVERSITY
PRESS, LONDON, BOMBAY, AND KARACHI, AND IN CANADA BY THE COPP
CLARK PUBLISHING CO. LIMITED, TORONTO

CONRAD AIKEN

REUEL DENNEY teaches at the University of Hawaii and at the East-West Center. His books, ranging from poetry to social criticism, include *The Lonely Crowd*, of which he is co-author.

⸏ Conrad Aiken

Eᴀʀʟʏ in his work Conrad Aiken wrote:

> There are houses hanging above the stars
> And stars hung under a sea.

These suave, unsettling lines from *Senlin: A Biography* (1918) suggest in miniature much of what was to follow. The world of these verses is no other than the round world on which we live. Man's visual logic, if he tries to extend it very far, is turned upside down by the gravitational logic of the globe. "Can the same be true of all of man's mental life?" Aiken seems to be asking. In that event our thoughts and feelings are subject to fields of force in which fall is flight and flight is fall and high and low are interchangeable. Aiken's work in both verse and prose is concerned with just such circularities and reversibilities and his success with them is the success of all his best writing.

In the late 1940's the American critic Lionel Trilling, in a troubled appraisal of his favored "liberal imagination," remarked that "The sense of largeness, of cogency, of the transcendence which largeness and cogency can give, the sense of being reached in our secret and primitive minds — this we virtually never get from the writers of the liberal democratic tradition at the present time." There are, however, grounds for considering the best of Aiken's work as having provided some of what Trilling said he could not usually find. That work has now extended over half a century and has encompassed haunting poetry, prophetic criticism, varied fiction, and journalism. He has been justly called, by Allen Tate, "one of the few genuine men of letters left."

5

Conrad Aiken was the first (1889) of three sons born to New England-bred William and Anna Aiken. His surname points to the Scotch blood he shares with his thematic and stylistic ancestor Poe. His birthplace, Savannah, Georgia, was the city in which his Harvard-trained father practiced medicine, and the family lived on one of those pleasant squares whose back alleys provided a playground for boys of the neighborhood, both black and white. When Aiken went to Harvard in the fall of 1907 he joined without being at first aware of it one of the most influential groups of writers and intellectuals in the twentieth century. The classes of 1910–15 matriculated, among others later famous, T. S. Eliot, John Reed, Walter Lippmann, E. E. Cummings, and Robert Benchley.

Since his graduation Aiken has pursued one of the most distinguished careers in his literary generation, capturing and holding from the time of his earliest publications to the present an audience in both England and the United States. Along with this there has been a broad and genial exchange with many of his most luminous contemporaries. Outspoken and often unfashionable in his public statements on literary affairs and reputations and sometimes waspishly bantering in his conversation on such matters, Aiken has nevertheless been blessed with a gift for friendship with his artistic peers. The public record of this is characterized by cooperation without hint of coterie machinations and controversy unmarked by tones of rancor. The mutual regard of Allen Tate and Conrad Aiken, for example, is some sort of monument to the transcendence by affection of deep differences in temperament and virtually diametrical perceptions of art and politics. Working to please himself, sometimes in New York, sometimes in Sussex or on Cape Cod, more recently in Georgia as well, Aiken has earned most of his living solely by writing and has memorialized his experiences in a remarkable autobiographical work of human and artistic self-analysis, *Ushant: An Essay* (1952).

Ushant, of which more must be said later, touches upon major aspects of Aiken's life and art: the unstinting dedication to poetry; the interest in psychoanalytic doctrine and "musical" form; the self-reversing attachments to the United States and England; the conscious continuance of a family tradition of liberalism and humanism; and the overcoming of tragedy in his early life. The third-person protagonist of *Ushant*, "D.," a reference to the character Demarest in the novel *Blue Voyage*, is a persona of Aiken himself and if there is such a thing as an interior-monologue autobiography of a literary man, perhaps *Ushant* is it. Indirectly candid in factual reference, it provides a Proustian regress toward the tragedy of Aiken's eleventh year (when both his parents died by the hand of the father, and he, "finding them dead, found himself possessed of them forever"). A high point is the scene in which the New England grandmother who has taken an interest in the orphaned D. gradually and tactfully brings his suicide father into the conversation, thus restoring the father to a place of conscious respect — and turns over the writings of the tragic man to the child so that the child can reach for identification with what was best in the father's life and work. Since it is these more profoundly personal aspects of *Ushant* that will monopolize our attention later on in this essay, it is necessary to notice here that the work has an important public interest as a chapter in modern literary history. Providing an informal commentary on literary men Aiken has known, it presents them in half disguises: Ezra Pound, for example, is "Rabbi Ben Ezra"; Eliot, the "Tsetse."

The global generality of the fragment quoted above from one of Aiken's earliest reputation-making poems might hint even to

a reader who has not yet read *Senlin* that he gives himself freely
to rhapsodizing forms. The play with incongruities, especially in
the complex concreteness with which the poet evokes a relativ-
ized viewpoint, seems to be a prevision of lines by Dylan Thomas:

> And I am dumb to tell a weather's wind
> How time has ticked a heaven around the stars . . .

Consider the masterly larger unit of verse containing the lines
quoted at the head of this essay:

> It is morning, Senlin says, and in the morning
> When the light drips through the shutters like the dew,
> I arise, I face the sunrise,
> And do the things my fathers learned to do.
> Stars in the purple dusk above the rooftops
> Pale in a saffron mist and seem to die,
> And I myself on a swiftly tilting planet
> Stand before a glass and tie my tie.
>
> Vine leaves tap my window,
> Dew-drops sing to the garden stones,
> The robin chirps in the chinaberry tree
> Repeating three clear tones.
>
> It is morning. I stand by the mirror
> And tie my tie once more.
> While waves far off in a pale rose twilight
> Crash on a coral shore.
> I stand by a mirror and comb my hair:
> How small and white my face! —
> The green earth tilts through a sphere of air
> And bathes in a flame of space.
>
> There are houses hanging above the stars
> And stars hung under a sea.
> And a sun far off in a shell of silence
> Dapples my walls for me.

(It should be noted that Aiken has sometimes made changes
in his poems before reprinting them in selected or collected

editions. The quotations included here are taken from the latest editions, for the most part from *Collected Poems* of 1953.)

Surely the young Aiken richly let himself go in *Senlin* and the other pieces — *The Charnel Rose* (1918), *The House of Dust* (1920), *The Jig of Forslin* (1921), *The Pilgrimage of Festus* (1923) — that make up *The Divine Pilgrim*, the long sequence of "symphonies" written in the years 1914 to 1920, when he was in his late twenties. The literary influences are unconcealed. Swinburne's tone had already been present in *Nocturne of Remembered Spring* (1917): "After long days of dust we lie and listen / To the silverly woven harmonies of rain . . ." *The Divine Pilgrim* shows Aiken as the rapt reader of others who had preceded him. Poe: "For seven days my quill I dipt / To wreathe my filigrees of script . . ." Browning: "Here's my knife — between my fingers I press it, / And into the panic heart . . . / Do you still hear the music? Do you still see me?" Wilde: "Death, among violins and paper roses . . ." As R. P. Blackmur says, Aiken's readiness to continue to call upon the conventional poetic vocabulary that he relied upon in this early work has remained with him all his life. At the same time the inventive advances he achieved in these pieces constitute some of his strongest claims to attention. *Forslin*, says Allen Tate, is the first poem in the English language in which a symphonic texture is employed to develop a philosophical theme. In this blend of the lyric and the narrative the lyric predominates and is centered on the feeling and thought of a single character.

These poems, besides showing how closely Aiken along with other *littérateurs* of his generation at Harvard studied Arthur Symons' *The Symbolist Movement in Literature* (1899), tell us much about what kind of an artist Aiken wished to be. A first clue is his interest in drawing upon music for suggestions about the forms of poems, an interest centered upon the capacity of music for presenting simultaneously several different levels of sound and meaning. This perhaps Wagnerian preoccupation with a thematic plurality of voices is directly connected, in turn, with Aiken's leading intuition of human character and circumstance. Influenced by the early psychoanalytic movement, Aiken sees man as a creature existing in both awareness and unawareness. The voices from the unawareness deserve to be rendered. But how? Aiken's solution is one that has now become conventional but was not always so. He makes these voices carry a symbolic content in which traditional and psychoanalytic motifs are blended. The manner is also what the composer might call "chromatic" and "impressionistic." It is worth noticing that although Aiken himself has made not a few references to the French Symbolists, he attached himself to them far less programmatically than some other American poets of his generation and his own style is that of impressionism — impressionism strongly tinged with that still older school that the French called Parnassian. Such predilections led him to produce poems whose strength lies in their brilliant and fulsome rendering of typical human temperaments. Let us consider his own analysis of his method.

In *Poetry Magazine*, in 1919, Aiken remarked that the arrangement of the four parts of *The Jig of Forslin* was such that Part IV gains, in its position, a certain effect it could gain at no other position in the sequence. Each emotional tone in the poem is employed like a musical tonality. "Not content to present emotions or things or sensations for their own sakes . . . this method takes only the most delicately evocative aspects of them, makes of them a keyboard, and plays upon them a music of which the chief characteristic is its elusiveness, its fleetingness, and its richness in the shimmering overtones of hint and suggestion." This idea of impressionistic musicality in poetry follows suggestions popularized by, among others, a writer who was a noticeable influence upon Aiken and his generation, Walter Pater. In his essay on "The School of Giorgione" Pater lent his elegant pen to the notion that any art (painting, for example) could learn from another art (music, for example, or literature) employing another sensuous medium and (somewhat contradictorily) that "all art constantly aspires to the condition of music."

Aiken himself sometimes used the word "chorus" in connection with his method. A character in the early poems is conceived as generating a wide-range band of voices from various levels and temporal sectors of the psyche; and the themes carried by these voices are elaborated in a sequence of variations somewhat in the way the composer undertakes the expansion and development of themes in a symphony or, perhaps more properly, a tone poem. While it is certainly true that Aiken's poems do have parts in which the mingled voices of many selves of the principal character seem to vocalize together in the same lines at the same time, the word "chorus" is not entirely satisfatory. The reason is that the various aspects of a character also are frequently rendered in a manner quite different from that of the chorus: it is a regular occurrence for them to appear in separate successive solos. The method is operatic or oratoric rather than choral, and might as well be called so.

Although Aiken referred to a "chorus" in the sense of its use as a musical rather than a dramaturgical device, there is a sense in which he could just as properly have emphasized the latter meaning. A trait of the chorus in an early Greek play was that it took a standpoint distinct from that of both the protagonist and the audience, serving as a narrative and meditative "we" disjoined from both. One of the expository advantages of this was that the chorus could be made to share information and feelings with the audience that were not made available to the protagonists, thereby generating one type of dramatic irony. There is a sense in which the voices emanating from the unawareness of the agent in a poem by Aiken serve similar purposes. The principal resemblance lies in the fact that these voices make available to the reader a certain knowledge of the agent not possessed by the agent himself. This involves the use of the now-familiar literary device best known as "interior monologue." Aiken early employed it in his poems to obtain a contrast between a character's conscious and unconscious motivations, thus effecting what we might term "psychoanalytic irony." It is not clear that Aiken himself was entirely aware of what he had hold of here. His comments on his own work do not fully identify the originality of a form he had discovered partly as a result of his interest in psychology.

Senlin is crucial to our analysis so far. A dreamlike poem, like a dream, represents the same relatively simple thing over and over again, whatever the disguises and semi-disclosures. What does *Senlin* represent and render? A poem influenced by Eliot's "The Love Song of J. Alfred Prufrock," it is concerned with a raw young man forced by his age and his character into a state of intense self-consciousness. On one level he is expressing and struggling with self-pity and a sense of isolation. On another he is expressing and struggling with solipsism. On both levels he is confronted with the problem of the relativity of perceptions and judgments. One of the results and signs of Senlin's crisis is the confusion between the stages of his life. While still not aged, he acts old, thus missing his youth. This habit of acting while young and raw as if he were older and more jaded is both the cause and the effect of his incomplete identity. A particular form taken by this crisis is the fear that he may be hurt by women or that this expectation will itself eventuate in his hurting them. When all sections of the poem are taken into account the basic statement of *Senlin* is this:

A young man keeps walking and climbing, with a feeling that he has been abandoned by the goal that is at the end of the road and the powers that are at the top of the stairs. He is returned incessantly to a situation in which he digs up a young woman.

This can be condensed:

A young man digs up a young woman.

This sentence states the whole dramatic meaning of *Senlin*: the ascent to the transcending other of a fatherly greater maleness, greater age, and wisdom is unsuccessful or at least difficult. Attempts to ascend to this are always accompanied or followed by rediscoveries of the dead traces of the non-male in the self. Senlin is too much like a woman to be a woman's lover. Yet the non-male in Senlin is not alive and active; it is, in every sense except recollection of it, dead.

When Aiken, in the early and middle 1920's, directed much of his attention toward fiction he marked, one might say, not only the beginning of a new kind of productivity but the end of a stage of the old. If Aiken had never collected more of his poems than those represented in the dozen or so that culminated in *Senlin*, he would have been assured of a place in twentieth-century American writing. In the period from the early twenties to 1940, however, Aiken completed not only new poems in new forms but also all of his novels, most of his short stories, and a fair share of his prose and criticism. The move into fiction had its adventurous elements as we shall see when we examine the work itself, but it may also have had its elements of necessity. Aiken was the father of three children by his first marriage (1912) and he remarried twice after that, once in 1930 and again in 1937. His own small patrimony was probably not adequate for these financial responsibilities and what he could earn by his pen was therefore crucial to him. Although Aiken never became a big seller in fiction his success in the field was not, to his gratification, solely an artistic one. Its artistic merits, however, along with its developmental place in his lifework, invite our attention now.

Few fictional works by a modern poet are as well known as Aiken's "Silent Snow, Secret Snow." A tapping into the stream of consciousness of a boy who appears to be relapsing into isolation and death wish, it is one of the best of the short stories in which Aiken has demonstrated his skill. Admiring Chekhov, James, and Andreyev, Aiken has worked mostly in the twentieth-century form of psychological fiction that we associate with Édouard Dujardin, Joyce, Dorothy Richardson, and Virginia Woolf. We should take special notice of Aiken's ability to repossess from the writers of fiction some of the tools they borrowed so readily from poets. The question of the relation between the poetry and the prose of Aiken might seem to be satisfied by referring to the blend of the symbolic and the psychological that we find in both. This reminiscence of the ambidextrous Poe is reinforced not by any interest of Aiken's in shrewd plotting but by his general attraction to the macabre and by the pleasure he sometimes takes in poetic texture as a resource of prose. Yet while most of Aiken's short stories offer complexity of character rather than plot they are not eventless. They ground themselves in those slowly gathering expectations that create suspense, provide the basis for dramatic reversal in the condition of the characters, and qualify the pieces as stories rather than portraits. The same is true of his novels.

Blue Voyage, earliest of his five novels, appeared in 1927. Returning to his ship's bunk each night, William Demarest recreates not only the events of the day and his expectations of the day to follow but also his deeper past. Does he possess a true identity — or rather, will the interactions of the voyage reveal one to him? This question is seen as pivoting on his chase of Cynthia, the girl of his past who has turned up as a passenger of the very ship on which he has sought to reach her in Europe. Aiken establishes a nice contrast between the sophistication ascribed to Demarest by his co-passengers and the abdominal Jello that is Demarest's other self, though he is probably dilatory in exploiting the comic possibilities in his portrait of a shipboard prig. As Demarest (which could be read as the Latin-like *de mare est,* "from the sea he is") comes toward the end of his voyage, having lost Cynthia even before the voyage began, we have been treated to episodes vitalized by an action whose course has described a circle.

Great Circle (1933) employs a massive flashback to explore two events separated in time by a generation. The later event is the protagonist's stealthy discovery of his wife's infidelity; the earlier is his parallel loss of childhood innocence when he is the witness of a tragic affair between his mother and his uncle. A sort of Harvard Square *Hamlet, Great Circle* is not so much a novel as a morality play in print, vexed by problems of viewpoint, tone, and central action. The binary pattern, in which each of the crises, past and present, is at once more important and less important than the other, is true enough to the temporal relativism of the twentieth century. But Aiken's symbolic loadings, such as the hero's loss of one eye — emblem perhaps of his Oedipal situation — seem arbitrary and distracting. The best section of the book is one in which the hero's Harvard classmate, who has alcoholically graduated into the status of a completely self-understanding and clairvoyant bum, provides an amateur psychoanalysis of the hero for an evening of drinks.

King Coffin (1935) is a descendant of Hogg, Poe, Stevenson, and Dostoevski and a predecessor of Camus' *The Stranger.* Jasper Ammen, the hero, has become obsessed with his observations of a stranger, Mr. Jones. Jones is unaware that Ammen has not only voyeuristically selected him for study but also elected him as the future victim of a gratuitous homicide. Told in roughly chronological sequence from a viewpoint somewhere "just back of" third-person protagonist Ammen, it shows us how Ammen's plan to commit the Raskolnikofian murder of the stranger, Jones, is reversed by the mournful birth of a stillborn baby to Mrs. Jones and its seemingly perfunctory burial. The death of the baby, by linking Jones with the banality of human life in general, disqualifies Jones as the pure and single stranger-victim of the crime. After the infant's burial, Ammen's desire to kill Jones evaporates, leaving Ammen himself as the only possible victim for the supreme jape in "Nietzschean" aggression that he has been cryptically telling his friends about.

In view of this construction, it might be thought that Aiken would foreshadow without revealing the unexpected appearance in Jones's life of a baby; but both the reader and Jasper Ammen become too early aware that a baby is to be born to the Joneses and this works against the force of the denouement. The convergence apparently intended between the simpler plot (Ammen's exposure of his vague plans to his confidants; his challenge to them to reveal those plans; and their alerting of his father) and the more complex plot (the transformation of Jones into a family- and life-connected person who cannot be defined as a pure ritual victim) does not fully work. Yet there are passages of remarkable success in the book. The experiments of Ammen with the air paths of the smoke of his cigarette signal to us, perhaps before Ammen himself knows it, that he is verging toward suicide by self-asphyxiation. Equally moving are the sections in which Aiken renders the succession of psychosomatic calms and storms through which Ammen passes on his way to final self-isolation and self-destruction.

These productions, along with *A Heart for the Gods of Mexico* (1939), with its quest motif, and the Cape Cod comedy *Conversation* (1940), with its portraiture of children, show that Aiken is the many-gifted literary man who turns with fascination, confidence, and professional energy toward current forms of fiction, and they demonstrate that he can work with them quite as well as many practitioners and better than most. (His one attempt to write a play, *Mr. Arcularis*, by turning a short story into a script, was not, however, a success.) He offers us no large-scale "Conrad Aiken World" of narrative prose but rather a winding "Post Road" through eastern American urban and suburban social scenes, passing through self-conscious counties connected with those of C. Brockden Brown in the past, Robert Coates among his contemporaries, and John Updike in the present. It is quite understandable that Aiken was one of the very first (in 1927, in a review in the *New York Post*) to recognize and raise significant questions about the genius of Faulkner.

Discussion of Aiken's fiction leads us naturally in the direction of his other major experiment in prose narrative, *Ushant*. Readers of this work meet in it the two principal masks of the artist-hero D. created by Aiken. The first is seeking the gratification he thinks he will be content with. The second is a gloomer bemoaning the loss of the gratification or its excessive price. The title itself indicates not only this polarity but others as well. Ushant is a dragon-shaped rock on the French side of the English Channel's opening into the Atlantic. Its associations include both departure and landfall, the idea of a westward limit to inquiry but also the notion of a taking-off place from Europe. This title was plainly offered in the expectation that it would be received as a Joycean transliteration of "You shan't" and as a metaphor both for the Ten Commandments and the superego. The work strives to render, by the expansion of a single state of the consciousness of D. (a moment in a steamer bunk, late in his life), the totality of D.'s struggle with the world and himself. The forward movement in time is left to be reconstructed by the reader from nonchronological recollections concerning three conscious goals of the writer's life: literary excellence, women's favors, and self-understanding.

This anthology of formative scenes in D.'s life is rendered with less clinical self-analysis than one might have tolerated and this has the advantage of leaving it up to the reader to complete the connections where he himself thinks they make sense. There is a chilling moment when D.'s mother comes to tuck him in as a child of seven or eight and asks him if, when he grows up, he will "protect her." This scene may point forward to D.'s family tragedy — and more than that; it may even foreshadow the episodes in the life of D. when his pursuit of women can be interpreted as a response to exorbitant demands made upon him as a child. A burden of comic complaint running through the book is that the searcher for art and love cannot attain both.

How are the disclosures of *Ushant* to be taken? If psychology is wrong or irrelevant about such lives as Aiken's or if Aiken is wrong or irrelevant about how it applies to them, the retrospection of *Ushant* produces not an autobiography but, as Jay Martin suggests, an art work half revealing and half veiling the life of an author — D. — *Ushant*'s author. On the other hand, if psychology is right and relevant about such lives as Aiken's and if Aiken is right and relevant about how it applies to them, the work has a kind of biographical weight over and beyond the artfulness of its portraiture. It seems appropriate here to assume that Aiken himself understood that *Ushant*'s readers would be pulled in the direction of both interpretations. Therefore, even if the reader inclines toward enjoying *Ushant* more as a literary artifact than as a biographical record he is compelled to have considered the latter dimension as a built-in aspect of the former. *Ushant*, it is clear, obliges us to take a much closer look at Aiken's relation to psychological teachings.

Aiken's first acquaintance with psychoanalytic thought was made while he was still an undergraduate at Harvard, around 1909, just about the time when Freud delivered to Americans his now-famous lectures at Clark University. From almost the beginning Aiken was regarded as an accomplished hanger-on of the movement, especially in the conversational games of "Latent Motive" and "Dream Analysis" as they were then practiced by devotees upon each other. As a consequence of Freud's admiration for Aiken's novel *Great Circle*, there was an opportunity for Aiken to be himself analyzed by Freud in Europe, with a friend offering the necessary financial aid. Aiken decided not to undertake the experiment. Years later, in *Ushant*, he wondered whether this might not have been a mistake. More or less characteristically, he could not make up his mind about the foregone opportunity. There is no doubt, however, that the fifth *Divine Pilgrim* "symphony," *The Pilgrimage of Festus*, has qualities that permit us to view Aiken as philosophical expositor as well as artistic exploiter of psychoanalytic views.

Aiken describes *Festus* as a study in "epistemology" and so it is. According to Freud, the cognitions of man are reshaped and distorted, as in a warped lens, by wishes that are the father to the thought. Festus, the hero, who is a kind of Faustus as well as a *Festung* (or fortress) and *festive*, is seen constructing a world out of his own "projections." Extending this theme to its limit, Aiken portrays Festus as a "paranoid" giving free rein in his fantasy and his actions to a sadistic vein. The whole poem is an exploration of the idea that knowledge is obtained when a Subject fully imposes itself upon an Object — the perception that Freud expressed by arguing that a surgeon's therapeutic violation of the body can be considered as the sublimation of an impulse originally cruel. Knowledge begins in hurting as well as wishing and willing and searching; and we had better recognize that systems of knowledge, being systematic, are also sadistic. As a remapping of the Faust legend, *Festus* implies the recognition of and recoil from the fact that scientific experiment sometimes is driven to contaminate its own object of research even to the point where, as in biology, it kills its specimens and thus denatures the nature it aims to study. Moreover Festus himself is, in effect, his own victim.

On the basis of what has been said so far, what can be suggested about the role of psychological theories in Aiken's life and in Aiken's work? To begin, some generalizations on the biography whose tragedy and triumph were sketched above:

First, Aiken's life story is quite unlike that of many of his artistic contemporaries who were also interested in Freud. The aberrations that in their families may have lain under the surface were in Aiken's family the conditions for a tragedy that was acted out to its end. Aiken, we can imagine, was drawn toward a general psychiatric interest in his own past more forcefully than most of his artistic contemporaries.

Second, his general psychiatric interest in his own past was stimulated by his knowledge of certain factors in his background, namely hereditary and organic ones, which happen to be, by definition, precisely the sort from which Freud withdrew his interest in the course of developing his nonsomatic theory of mental disorder. We are told in *Ushant*, for example, that

Aiken's mother and father were cousins, and there are remarks in the work suggesting that Aiken was aware that he may have inherited a strain of petit mal, the milder form of epileptic seizure.

Third, Aiken's active response to the threatening disorders of the period of his latency had probably already brought him to a certain state of mental health before he ever heard of Freud.

Fourth, the "Oedipal conflict" in Aiken's life was presumably left uncompleted in Freud's terms because of his father's self-removal from the family scene while Aiken was between eleven and twelve. The same act that deprived the child of the conflict also deprived him of his mother, the conflict's prize.

It is Aiken himself, in *Ushant*, who provides the data of these four speculations. In this situation it would be irresponsible for us to follow certain valuable self-denying ordinances of modern criticism. What is required is precisely what these ordinances forbid: the pursuit of clinical themes in the work and the linkage of these themes with the makeup of the writer. Given the four biographical conditions of Aiken's relationship to psychological doctrines, it can be suggested that one would not expect to find in Aiken's work a fully developed concern with Freud's Oedipus theme. Nor do we. It also follows that a generally psychiatric, as opposed to specifically psychoanalytic, concern for his own past would be at work in Aiken. The psychoanalytic interest would arise only when he had to consider the consequences for his own identity of having been deprived of the Oedipal conflict. This is noticeable also. Although there are hints of the Oedipal theme in *Senlin* (II, 8), it is broached more overtly in *Blue Voyage*, when Aiken's hero relocates his girl Cynthia only to learn that she is already engaged to be married. Read "mother" for "Cynthia" and the Oedipal rivalry theme is complete. It also turns up in *Mr. Arcularis*, in which an uncle is substituted for a father as the mother's lover. It appears in somewhat the same form in *Great Circle*. In all these references, the weight of the Oedipal theme is not heavy and the emphasis is almost entirely on the jealous search for possession of the mother, hardly at all on the direct struggle with the father. Although *King Coffin* portrays an open enmity between father and son, it is offered chiefly as one of the explanatory conditions of subsequent events and is not much dwelt upon in itself. The poems, the prose, and *Ushant* all suggest that this weighting reflects Aiken's own life and preoccupations. Even D.'s discovery later in his life that he had been taking his rebelling grandfather as a model can be interpreted as a conventional and mild critique of D.'s father.

This does not exhaust, however, the relationships joining Aiken's biography, his psychologizing, and his work. In a section of *Ushant*, D. recalls a picture drawn of him in early infancy by his father. Retrospection tells him that in this portrait his father showed an infant possessing godlike self-assurance. The passage implies that the picture dramatizes the father's recoil before the potential power of his first child, a male. After such infantile omnipotence, what innocence? D.'s comment is simple, brilliant, and touched by Mark Twain: "That child's father and mother were already as good as dead" — a boldly ironic apology for being born. Here Aiken seems to acknowledge both as doctrine and as indirect biography the idea that the son of a father who has killed himself may sometimes feel the event as the materialization of his own wish. It is not odd therefore that the themes and situations developed by Aiken in his early work involve fantasies of horrid actions, nightmares capable of serving to rationalize a guilt already felt. One fantasy after another is tested in order to see which one fits best a pre-established mood of guilt. *The Charnel Rose* explores survivals of the "infantile polymorphous perverse"; *Forslin,* the autistic stages of mentality; *Senlin,* the homosexual identification of self; *Festus,* "paranoid" sadism. Later, in *Punch* (1921), Aiken explored another face of sadism.

Since our major interest here is directed not toward Aiken's life but toward his writing, the foregoing speculations can be useful to us chiefly because they suggest how Aiken's psychologizing influenced his self-definition as an artist. The identification of five characteristics seems in order here. First of all, his intellectual appeal to psychological doctrine as a clue to the meaning in life. Second, his concern with substitutes or "surrogates" in human experience — Aiken early wrote of himself as having an interest in "the process of vicarious experience by which civilized man enriches his life and maintains emotional balance." Third, his employment of a "musical" method in verse composition, a method which emphasizes the associative stream of imagery both in the minds of the characters represented and in the compositional habits of the writer. Fourth, his exploration of themes of ego, identity, and the "defense mechanisms." Fifth, his use of phallic symbolism in a manner suggesting that the reader can be expected to possess a knowledge of that code. The doctrinal details of these concerns dominated Aiken less and less as he matured.

Despite these conjectures pressed upon our attention by the masquerade of *Ushant* it will occur to many readers of Aiken that even if his life experiences had been different, his art might have demonstrated the same concerns; and that, for readers who know nothing or who could not care less about his life, the poems present themselves not as fragmented history but as the make-believe of art. It follows that they make a claim to be concerned with the destiny of all men rather than one man alone and that this exploration of the general as opposed to the particular involves an examination of the evils that all men encounter and a search for sources of value that all men can share. In effect, this involves a research into the depths of universal guilt, conscience, and indeed the sense of human solidarity. Aiken's approach to these matters deserves greater clarification than it has as yet received.

Lest what needs to be said about this seem to make Aiken a rhetorician rather than a poet it would be well to look for a moment at how well Aiken defended the claims of art in his criticism as well as in his poetry. For the intellectual background of Aiken's beliefs about the relation between life and art presents itself quite clearly in his criticism, not because it is programmatic but because, despite its range, it is consistent and coherent in its drive. Aiken undertook considerable reviewing, much of it at the behest of Marianne Moore for the *Dial*, and his criticism has the vitality of taste-in-the-making. It is rather to its credit that his is not the sort of criticism that labors first of all to pre-establish a position of defense for the writer's own poetry. Nor does it rework ground already covered by others. One could summarize its strength by noticing Aiken's early perception of grandiose confusions in Pound. To get an idea of Aiken's range and perception as a critic one has to turn only to *Scepticisms* (1919), in which he writes freely and incisively about himself as well as his contemporaries. More realistically, since *Scepticisms* has long been difficult to come by, one should take advantage of Rufus Blanshard's service to Aiken's reputation by examining his *A Reviewer's ABC*, a 1958 publication which reprints most of the pieces on which Aiken is willing to rest his critical reputation. As displayed in the *ABC*, the ranginess and independence of this work calls up Hazlitt and Baudelaire; and what may most distinguish it is the magnanimity by which it rises above the professional animus and often intrusive pedantry that burden much of the criticism in English that has appeared in the twentieth century. A most perceptive and helpful commentary on Aiken's development as a critic is provided by Jay Martin. According to Martin, Aiken's early attitude toward literature leaned toward that of Tolstoi in *What Is Art?* The stress was placed upon the moral effects of the artist upon his audience. Later, Martin tells us, Aiken gradually articulated quite a different position, one that gave rather more attention to the artist as autonomous explorer of reality. Perhaps it would be fair to say of this process that Aiken has given up Tolstoi in order to replace him with Croce. Yet even though Aiken's criticism leans closer and closer to a Crocean core as it proceeds, it does not forsake all sense of the instruction that is found in art, and may even, like his poetry, constitute more of a teaching than Aiken has been prepared to admit.

We should keep in mind these aspects of Aiken's attitude toward the poetic art as we try to come closer to an understanding of how Aiken involved himself in poetry as a channel of total feeling and thinking. In the "symphonies" Aiken undertook to study the engulfing vice or virtue of a human temperament from the point of view of new scientific doctrines about such matters. While the background of this can be seen extending from Aristotle and Theophrastus to Ben Jonson and La Bruyère, the particular intellectual source of Aiken's "symphonies" is the interest in characterology handed forward by such men as Wilhelm Dilthey from early nineteenth-century philosophies to Freud, Spranger, Scheler, Jung, Fromm, and Erikson. This line of thought is concerned quite as much with "identity" as with "personality" and it includes a consideration of ethical problems. Since Aiken is true to this tradition — the moral worth of a character such as that of Senlin is studied in the poem in the light of his perilous preoccupation with himself — it is hard to understand the habit of minimizing the moralist in Aiken. But it appears that there are two reasons for this judgment, one involving a development in philosophy and one involving Aiken's manner of constructing the moral orientation of his characters.

The first, or philosophical, consideration is that we have witnessed a narrowing of the province of ethics in Great Britain and the United States since the turn of the century. This is seen in the tendency of ethics to pursue "normative" as contrasted with "descriptive" inquiry. For philosophers following such men as Bradley and McTaggart and for critics such as Eliot and Winters, a system of ethics appears to be validated largely by showing that it is entailed by the nature of an ultimate reality. But this can only be an article of faith rather than philosophy, since no system of ethics can be validated merely by this warrant. Besides, there are those who hold that descriptive as well as deductive inquiry is required in ethics; and Aiken is one of these. The source of ethics that others seek in an intuition of duty to a metaphysical realm Aiken seeks in an intuition of human purposes in the realm of nature; and his poems constitute a teaching in this ancient tradition of moral judgments — a tradition which is as evident to us in Epicurus and Lucretius as it is in Freud. And if we pursue this line of investigation more fully we shall see why Aiken employs a particular and significant method for developing the moral orientation of his characters.

David Bakan, in one of the chapters of his work in progress on modern psychology, has called attention to the power of dynamic psychology as a system of metaphor. He suggests that thought is renewed from time to time by revolutions in its systems of metaphor and that not the least of Freud's contributions was of just this sort. This is one of the principal ways in which Aiken understood psychoanalysis and it is a way that is not yet grasped by many who claim to understand Freud. Along similar lines John Chynoweth Burnham, in one of the chapters in his forthcoming study of the intellectual climate in which modern psychiatry arose, notes that Edwin B. Holt of Harvard, in *The Freudian Wish and Its Place in Ethics*, as early as 1915 saw Freud as translator into modern terms of the idea that knowledge, including knowledge of self, is a virtue. Aiken read this book when it first appeared. Scattered throughout Aiken's work, including *Osiris Jones* (1931) and *Preludes for Memnon* (1931), appear systematic comments along this line. Aiken's Freudian belief in the determination of all mental life by all of its past did not make him a psychological determinist in the sense that Hardy was an environmental determinist and Dreiser a naturalistic determinist. Rather it encouraged him to develop the voluntarism and relativism of his minister grandfather's dissenting brand of the Unitarian view.

As a consequence Aiken moved from the very beginning toward views of human nature that stand in contrast to comparable concerns in many of his artistic contemporaries. For them the center of interest is the family as the source of an oppressive cultural superego and they seek a new compact with the guilt they believe has been forced upon them by their upbringing. Aiken on the other hand is concerned with the development of ego in situations in which the outside world must be substituted for the family. From the outset, therefore, he is led in the direction of an interest in character disorders rather than the neurotic or the psychotic. The questions he asks himself are more like those asked by a psychoanalyst such as Harry Stack Sullivan, with his sensitivity to social aspects of personality, than like those of earlier and more "classical" masters of the field. By accident and insight Aiken anticipated the interest in "identity" as contrasted with the interest in "personality" that appeared in fullest form in the American school of Freudian revisionists. Aiken's relationships to dynamic psychology are therefore about as different as they can be from the picture of them provided by some critics of Aiken's work such as Peterson, Martin, and Hoffman and even by some opaque remarks in Aiken himself. "The cosmic ironist" in Aiken pivots not so much upon a struggle of personality for a place in an impersonal cosmos as upon the struggle of the human being, over and beyond being possessed of a "personality," to arrive at an identity.

Consider the persistence of this theme in the eloquent late poem "The Crystal":

> At seven, in the ancient farmhouse,
> cocktails sparkle on the tray, the careful answer
> succeeds the casual question, a reasoned dishevelment
> ruffling quietly the day's or the hour's issue.
> Our names, those we were born with,
> or those we were not born with, since all are born nameless,
> become the material, or the figment, if we wish,
> of which to weave, and then unweave, ourselves.
> Our lives, those we inherited, of which
> none can claim ownership in fee simple, but only
> a tenant's lease, of unpredictable duration,
> rented houses from which have already departed perhaps
> those others, our other selves, the children . . .

It is important to notice that whereas Frost's Social Darwinism and Eliot's anthropology and Pound's culture-history have all dated, Aiken's psychology anticipated forty years ago a major viewpoint in psychology today. We do not dismiss writers for the obsolescence of the intellectual fashions that once nourished them any more than we praise them for their anticipation of scientific world-views. On the other hand we can praise them for the coherence with which a unified view of man is dramatized in, and dramatizes, their work. On this score Aiken displays an intelligent consistency that makes some contemporaries of his, for example Pound, sound incoherent and others, for example Stevens, seem bloodless. Thus, in analyzing how Aiken's view of man led him to undertake certain crucial experiments in form we dare not fail to evaluate what he says about man and for man — all the more so because Aiken has avoided the role of guru accepted for themselves by some of his best known contemporaries.

With this observation, however, we are brought close to a crucial question not only for Aiken but for others in his generation. It is ordinarily expressed in the following terms: does the twentieth-century poet inherit a set of beliefs that make the triumphs and the failures of men significant? A set of beliefs that, because they are general beliefs about human action, assist the artist to portray human actions as possessing a sharp contour, against a clear-cut ground? The question develops some of its importance out of the observation that even poets such as Eliot or Claudel who have attached themselves to the authoritative belief system of traditional Catholicism have not been able to present in verse or in drama anything so artistically clear-cut as the doctrine itself claims to be in dogmatic terms. It develops further importance out of the observation that an artist who, like Brecht, has attached himself to the doctrinaire prophecies of Marx, has not been more convincing than the traditionalists as a dramatizer of man's good and evil. Aiken did not escape such difficulties by his attachment to a psychological liberalism that, if anything, supplies even less dramatizable contrast in human affairs. Even if it be true that classical Freudianism "rescues" for us some of what we still possess of the dramatic and the tragic, Aiken has not chosen that line of psychoanalytic thought. He has chosen rather an outlook that de-emphasizes contrast between absolute good and absolute evil, and disqualifies traditional hard-line distinctions between passion and action. The more experienced, anguished, and pessimistic version of this viewpoint, with its simultaneous rejection of Greek beliefs in fate, Christian assurance of salvation, and revolutionary expectations of a new social order, is probably to be found in such a continental writer as Camus. Aiken's version of it, like that of most Americans who espouse it, is not so pessimistic as the European and contains as a major element its radical rejection of two leading American intellectual traditions of the nineteenth century: the earlier Scottish realism, with its inadequate account of the human emotions, and the later Kantianism, with its glowing assurances that the universal law outside of man was reflected in, and reflected, the moral law within him.

Such a world-view multiplies the difficulties of the literary artist in his attempt to objectify and dramatize the moral orientation of the characters he is representing. One reason, suggested and developed recently by the philosopher Maurice Mandelbaum in *The Phenomenology of Moral Experience*, is that in making judgments of the moral worth of fictional characters as well as real people we make a distinction between two situations. One occurs when we make a judgment of an agent's "actional" traits; in this situation we can pass a judgment upon the action without second thoughts about the motive. The other appears when, in passing a judgment upon his action, we dare not dismiss the agent as lacking this or that moral attribute without inquiring into his motives and thus into the history of his relationship to the action. Aiken, in the "symphonies" and in *Punch*, invites us to judge his characters almost entirely in the latter terms and hardly at all in the former. Each character, that is, is like a delinquent standing before a liberal-minded judge: nothing that he has thought or done is to be judged independently of the temperament or disposition he evinces and represents. Aiken, whose true interest is in character and identity rather than personality and ego, achieves by this approach a singular power in the rendering of certain character types. The price of the method is shown, however, by the difficulties Aiken experienced in going from the portrait-poem and lyric to the narrative poem.

Aiken's biggest experiments with the narrative poem came toward the beginning and after the end of his novel-writing years, in *John Deth* (1930) and *The Kid* (1947).

John Deth follows its subtitle, *A Metaphysical Legend*, in being too complex. Inspired in part by the names on an English tombstone and in part by Aiken's Jungian advertence to the idea of mankind's collective dreaming, it draws on medieval myth. Aiken's own commentary on the genesis and the aim of the poem multiplies the difficulties of the piece. Yet it can be read with great enjoyment, as Jay Martin reads it, as a derivation from the dance of death allegorics, with a dreamlike persuasiveness and a certain narrative get-up-and-go.

The Kid is Aiken's contribution to the "lyric-epic" tradition that began in the United States with Whitman, was continued by Crane and Williams, and is also represented in sequences of the later Stevens. In this poem William Blackstone (inexplicable man who was willing to be Boston's first settler) is seen transmogrified into a sequence of American heroes in search of an inner frontier that is related to but not identical with the physical and national frontier to the westward. The poem owes as much to Owen Wister and Theodore Roosevelt as it does to Hart Crane and William Carlos Williams. *The Kid* contains wonderfully sustained passages, concludes with less than the obsessive brilliance of Crane's *The Bridge* or the pawky mythography of Williams' *Paterson*. The truth is that few poems of Aiken's force us to construct their protagonists so fully that we see and hear them ever after. His poems are not intended in this way any more than Ovid's or Spenser's poems are. The most persistently narrative efforts in Aiken's poetic work are aimed at representing an adventurous and problematic pursuit as it is undertaken by an allegorized temperament.

Aiken's definitely mixed accomplishments with narration and dramatization in verse pivot, as has been said, upon the difficulties inherent in moving from a poetic form that achieves a lyrical rendering of a character type whose actions and whose thoughts constantly flow into each other to a poetic form in which a character — since he exists among other characters — must be objectified clearly as someone who actually exists in the viewpoint of those other characters. A better understanding of how this familiar challenge presented itself to Aiken is obtained by examining more closely than we have so far the methods of composition that he employed in the early ground-breaking "symphonies." It can be shown that these methods were largely as successful as they were ingenious — but that they also entrenched habits that exerted a limiting influence upon Aiken's later experiments in narrative.

In those important early long poems that Aiken called "symphonies" the unit next largest to the whole is a section headed by a subtitle (or in some cases by a Roman numeral) that deals pretty much with one emotional tone or one emotional episode. This unit is perhaps the "movement" of the "symphony." The next smaller unit of composition is a group of traditional stanzas separated from their surroundings by an Arabic numeral, or by a space, from similar units before and after it. This unit, in turn, is composed of subsections fairly tightly unified by rhythm and by coterminous grammatical units. These subsections, written generally in lines of end-stopped character, are frequently enough made up of lines in couple, triple, or quadruple formation; each succeeding line undertakes to develop by repetition or variation a theme stated in the opening line. Here are examples of the part-Imagist, part-Biblical manner:

> Things mused upon are, in the mind, like music,
> They flow, they have a rhythm, they close and open,
> And sweetly return upon themselves in rhyme.

> *The Jig of Forslin,* I, 7

> Rain slowly falls in the bitter garden;
> It rains: the streets grow dark.
> The leaves make a sorrowful sound in the hidden garden;
> It rains, and the streets grow cold.

> *The Charnel Rose,* II, 2

This crucial smaller unit of Aiken's prosodic and poetic organization which I have called the "subsection" seems to me to be the fundamental building block of most of Aiken's poetry. As it is seen in the early work, it possesses an expressive unity reinforced not only by anaphora and other types of repetition but also by its formation around a unified cluster of sensuous impressions. Within this basic unit Aiken increasingly learned to build up such variations upon imagery that certain other features of its construction pass unnoticed. Of all the figurative devices that Aiken employs, one of his favorites is the substitution of a sign associated with one sense for a sign associated with another sense: synesthesia. Made both famous and fashionable by Baudelaire's sonnet "Correspondences," this device has been exploited by Aiken in ways that are particularly his own. Emphasizing the mutual substitution of the auditory and the visual, he also likes to play the natural and the artificial off against each other. Thus, when he makes reference under the auditory component to a natural sound such as the sound of rain, he likes to make reference under the visual component to something artifi-

cial; when he makes reference under the auditory component to
an artificial sound, such as the note of a trumpet, he likes to
make reference under the visual component to something as
natural as the shape of a flower. This is why, for example, the
interchange of the visual and the auditory in the opening movement of the title poem from *And in the Hanging Gardens* (1933)
speaks for him so typically:

> And in the hanging gardens there is rain
> From midnight until one, striking the leaves
> And bells of flowers, and stroking boles of planes,
> And drawing slow arpeggios over pools,
> And stretching strings of sound from eaves to ferns.

Now the more we read early Aiken the more we notice the
single-cast construction of his subsections. But what do single-
cast, coupled- and tripled-line structures have to do, even in
freely unrhymed fashion, with poems of the kind that Aiken said
he wished to write? Is the unconscious so tidy? Would not the
movements of the psyche with which Aiken claims to deal render themselves more persuasively in line and sentence arrange-
ments less sweetly formal than this? The dependence on end-
stopped clusters of lines in the subsections of the "symphonies"
introduces a prosodic formality that forfeits some of the
gains made by abandoning formal stanza patterns. Such early
critics of Aiken as Blackmur and Winters, it is to be guessed,
felt not only an over-smooth, redundant, and even cloying tone
in some of Aiken but also this related problem in the prosody
of the "symphonies." We can safely say, in any event, that this
method and texture is even less adaptable to the requirements
of narrative verse than it is to those of the symphonic poem.
The reason is that although it may facilitate the force of single-
character portraiture by repetition, variation, and expansion, it
does not contribute to narrative what narrative needs: the deft

34

introduction to the reader of distinguishable characters and the rapid rendering of events linked to each other in time and in causality.

Clearly a question of language in general, as well as the question of the figurative and prosodic modalities in smaller basic parts of Aiken's poetry, presents itself to us here. It is probably fair to say that during the years of Aiken's greatest poetic productivity a general debate was proceeding on questions of poetic diction. To a large extent the issues were lexical rather than, as they tend to be today, structural. That is to say, the poetic practitioner or critic examining, say, a poem by Robert Frost paid somewhat more attention to the general choice of usage, idiom, and word than to the ways by which Frost deployed the underlying intonational patterns that reinforce the sense of English in order to place his emphasis precisely where he wanted it to be in the line or verse-paragraph. Most discussion of Aiken's "texture" focuses its attention therefore on such lexical questions as his unmodish pleasure in adjectives and his willing dependence upon verbal constructions which had first been made expressive and then stereotyped by the progress of Romantic literary experiment. The point is not an unreasonable one even though it probably has been overemployed as a critique of Aiken's style. Since such observations have been a staple of Aiken criticism for a long time, it is necessary here only to acknowledge them and to suggest that other dimensions of Aiken's language are equally worthy of study: his sentence, for example.

The sentence in which Aiken achieves his cadence is the familiar informal declarative run-on sentence of American speech, made rather more formal in most respects than speech itself — Aiken is as free with the artful and unvernacular flourish ("This is the shape of the leaf and this of the flower") as any poet of his time. Generally, it is his habit to use a fairly loose sentence, adding clause upon clause in an unperiodic structure that follows the pulse of association as waves follow each other to a shore. The grammatical antecedents sometimes grow vague, and a natural accompaniment of this sentence is a good deal of anaphora and echolalia, as if the propulsion of feeling could be renewed from point to point only by associative returns to climaxes previously passed:

> It is morning, Senlin says, and in the morning
> When the light drips through the shutters like the dew,
> I arise, I face the sunrise,
> And do the things my fathers learned to do.

Little in the sentence structure of Aiken achieves a tension between what is carried in a principal clause and what is carried in a subordinate clause. The compound-complex organization, with its emphasis upon the compound, simply takes the form of refined rumination as it reaches the level of speech, adapting itself readily to the compulsive repetition that Aiken emphasizes in his rendering of the movement of human feelings. Anticlimax in this mode of composition is related to the employment of underconnected independent clauses that prevails in Hemingway ("He swung the axe and the chicken was dead") and Eliot ("Six o'clock. / The burnt-out ends of smoky days").

The language Aiken worked out for himself is the result of imitation, intuition, and trial and error. Successful though it is, it is far from being the sophisticated product of a "structural-linguistic" talent such as we find in Cummings and Thomas, remaining by and large at the conventional and lexical level characteristic of American linguistic thinking before, say, Leonard Bloomfield. It is a mistake to take Aiken's own somewhat ponderous comments on the "problem of language" as evidence for a keen philosophical or technically informed sense of the matter. They add little to our understanding and critical attention to them adds even less. The main thing to notice is Aiken's William Jamesian determination to let the thought think itself — and to stand by the consequences of the experiment. In his more ventriloquistic constructions the reader does not always know who is speaking or from what situation or from what context. The separation of the author and the fictional agent and the separation of the situation from the agent's sense of it has little of the clarity with which these matters are represented, in, for example, Frost. Nor are they necessarily intended to. The purpose of Aiken's style as well as of his total construction is to evoke mood and character and not to dramatize. It pictures, and it expatiates upon what has been pictured; and it represents what a character dreamed or wished or hoped as being on somewhat the same level as what he did or had done to him.

It was a tincture of cosmic purple among other things that was responsible for some of the bad reviews Aiken received in the 1920's — and even later, when it had become more frequent to speak of him as being overdetached from social values. It appears that points were sometimes missed about the earlier poems. It will help us to understand this if we go back for a moment to the famous earlier "Discordants" (*Turns and Movies*, 1916):

> Music I heard with you was more than music,
> And bread I broke with you was more than bread;
> Now that I am without you, all is desolate;
> All that was once so beautiful is dead.

The effect of "Discordants" arises partly from a trochaic foot in which the sharpest stresses combined with the highest pitches are placed toward the end of each line, to be reinforced there by the terminal junctures. It also depends upon alliterations and consonances attached to these strong-stressed and high-pitched syllables; and upon the placement toward the line end of most of the consonantal collisions heard in the poem, almost all of them bringing together smoothly a voiced consonant (a consonant requiring the voice box to vibrate, such as "b" contrasted with "p") with another of the same kind. The smoothness of the piece suggested to some that this was about the best that Aiken could do with English prosody — and that perhaps he had "done" too much.

But surely this was grudging praise and Aiken after 1930 forced a gradual reversal of such judgments by the meditative poems of *Preludes for Memnon*, *Time in the Rock*, and *Brownstone Eclogues*. In these poems he pursued the verbal refinement of all that he had learned before — and much that was new. This movement away from the quasi-dramatic or narrative is reinforced and enriched by Aiken's gradual discovery of freer variations and part of the excitement of the *Preludes* is our participation in Aiken's finding of new rhythms. The Wagnerian brass line of the earlier poems is transposed for woodwinds; and although the lines are still heavily end-stopped, the freedom and variation seem both effortless and endless as if from a self-renewing source:

> Watch long enough, and you will see the leaf
> Fall from the bough. Without a sound it falls:
> And soundless meets the grass . . . And so you have
> A bare bough, and a dead leaf in dead grass.
>
> *Preludes for Memnon*, XIX

Consider also this section:

> Two coffees in the Español, the last
> Bright drops of golden Barsac in a goblet,
> Fig paste and candied nuts . . . Hardy is dead,
> And James and Conrad dead, and Shakspere dead,
> And old Moore ripens for an obscene grave,

And Yeats for an arid one; and I, and you —
What winding sheet for us, what boards and bricks,
What mummeries, candles, prayers, and pious frauds?
You shall be lapped in Syrian scarlet, woman,
And wear your pearls, and your bright bracelets, too,
Your agate ring, and round your neck shall hang
Your dark blue lapis with its specks of gold.
And I, beside you — ah! but will that be?
For there are dark streams in this dark world, lady,
Gulf Streams and Arctic currents of the soul;
And I may be, before our consummation
Beds us together, cheek by jowl, in earth,
Swept to another shore, where my white bones
Will lie unhonored, or defiled by gulls.

Preludes for Memnon, II

It should be evident by this point that Aiken speaks in terms of a creed, liberalism, which has been on the defensive among the most inquiring poetic minds of the past two generations. He has written, to be sure, in terms of not classical political economic liberalism but rather the social-psychological liberalism which since the 1880's has rejected that earlier laissez-faire liberalism almost as much as it rejects absolutism. The coherence of creed and art in Aiken is rather more noticeable than it is in many of his contemporaries. Yet Aiken's own vaguenesses as well as the development of psychological doctrine in his own lifetime are probably responsible for some of the oversimplified views of the Freudianism that was a formative element in his art, liberalism, and relativism. It has not yet been said clearly enough that the classical Oedipus complex plays a minor part in his work; that his early interest in the ego and identity as over against the theory of complexes distinguishes his work utterly from the Freudian rhetoric of Robinson Jeffers and Eugene O'Neill; that, despite his interest in characterology, his poems have rarely received the "Freudian reading" that they deserve; that for better or worse (some think better), his Freud approaches the Freud of the "revisionists"; and that despite his reputation as a poet of chaos his work embodies a total, consistent, and normative view of man.

The orientation is visible in the earliest accomplished work. Certain common tones in Pound's "Hugh Selwyn Mauberley" (1915), Aiken's *The Jig of Forslin* (1916), and Eliot's "The Love Song of J. Alfred Prufrock" (1917) remind us of what these writers shared with each other. The central figure of each is a self-involved man out of tune with his warring time and not getting any younger. He is sketched by a method that recalls Browning's dramatic soliloquy while at the same time it deliberately disarranges this form toward impressionistic vagueness and Symbolist mystery. *Forslin,* because it includes a version of the Salome story in its middle passages, invites special attention to that theme. Mallarmé's poem *Hérodiade,* followed by a short tale by Flaubert, a prose poem of Huysmans, a novel by Sudermann, an opera by Strauss, paintings by Moreau, and a verse play by Oscar Wilde, show a preoccupation with the theme at the century's turn. Developing the vampire figure of Romantic writing, this motif became a flaming fashion during a time when the feminist movement was acquiring respectability and effectiveness and it touches on the discomfiture of the male in a period when he was continuing to lose his traditional dominance. Appearing almost simultaneously in "Prufrock" and *Forslin,* the theme helps us to understand the differences in the effects of the two poems.

In both poems an analogy is suggested between the absence of masculine initiative in love and the absence of the ability to experience, feel, and create. In Eliot's version we see the male dismissed or even victimized by the female and his own attitude toward her; and the whole relationship is passionately embalmed from an ironic and comic point of view. In Aiken's version we see the female told off by the male in a series of fantasies in which the male counter-anticipates the power of the female; and the whole relationship is rehearsed from a more or less melodramatic and pathetic point of view. Just as there is something like a European *tedium vitae* in the attitude taken by Eliot toward the battle of the sexes, there is something "contrary" and American about Aiken's choice of the other attitude. Not apart from these perspectives, the reader of today is likely to feel that Eliot, by going in the direction of ironic and comic treatment, attained somewhat greater control over his material than Aiken but also that he played it more or less safe by taking the myth at its inherited value.

Given these strategic choices that Aiken made when young, the important thing is that the poetic gifts he brought to them attained a richer and more controlled form when he was older. Consider this poem, "Doctors' Row" (in the *Brownstone Eclogues* of 1942):

Snow falls on the cars in Doctors' Row and hoods the headlights;
snow piles on the brownstone steps, the basement deadlights;
fills up the letters and names and brass degrees
on the bright brass plates, and the bright brass holes for keys.

Snow hides, as if on purpose, the rows of bells
which open the doors to separate cells and hells:
to the waiting-rooms, where the famous prepare for headlines,
and humbler citizens for their humbler deadlines.

And in and out, and out and in, they go,
the lamentable devotees of Doctors' Row;
silent and circumspect — indeed, liturgical;
their cries and prayers prescribed, their penance surgical.

No one complains — no one presumes to shriek —
the walls are very thick, and the voices weak.
Or the cries are whisked away in noiseless cabs,
while nurse, in the alley, empties a pail of swabs.

Miserable street! — through which your sweetheart hurries,
lowers her chin, as the snow-cloud stings and flurries;
thinks of the flower-stall, by the church, where you
wait like a clock, for two, for half-past two;

thinks of the roses banked on the steps in snow,
of god in heaven, and the world above, below;
widens her vision beyond the storm, her sight
the infinite rings of an immense delight;

all to be lived and loved — O glorious All!
Eastward or westward, Plato's turning wall;
the sky's blue streets swept clean of silent birds
for an audience of gods, and superwords.

Explorations of Aiken led by Blackmur and Tate and later
by Schwarz, Blanshard, Martin, and Hoffman have laid the
foundations for a fuller view of his work. Aiken is the poetic,
less carapaced, side of the American mentality of his generation that represents itself on the more intellectualized and dis-
cursive side in the confident criticism of Edmund Wilson. As
artist and as man, he displays an affection for the very world
that he attacks for being too distinct a giver of pain, too un-
certain a giver of pleasure, and too monstrous to be grasped by
a divided consciousness. His perception of suffering is not
Christian, or Nietzschean, or tragic, or skeptical, or withdrawing.
It is liberal, ironic, humane, conscious of the discontents that
civilization itself imposes and therefore relativistic and partly
hopeful. It is probably inconsistent for those who emphasize in
Aiken a sympathy for the Freudian formula of the "pathology
of everyday life" to see him as a poet of clear-cut pessimism
about personality or culture. There is to be found in Aiken as
well as in Freud the belief that "Where id was, there shall ego
be" — enough of a commitment to a rationalistic hope to leave
major aspects of Freud's thought and Aiken's poetry this side of

tragedy. Of all the themes that Aiken inherits from Freud, he emphasizes the one that is "non-tragic" in the inherited sense of the word, but painful enough in its human meaning: the quietest life, devoid of tragic incident or suffering, is already the victim of the internalized aggression that, in the form of conscience, punishes gratuitously the psyche that it inhabits.

This almost Baudelairian theme of the "heroism of everyday life" was well realized in "Tetélestai," written in 1917, when Aiken was twenty-eight. The title, drawn from the last words of Jesus in John 19:30 ("When Jesus therefore had received the vinegar, he said, It is finished; and he bowed his head, and gave up the ghost"), has the meaning, in John, of fulfillment as well as conclusion. An elegy for the obscure heroes of everyday life, this poem of Aiken's calls up a line like that of Marlowe to decorate the theme that Gray's *Elegy* is remembered for and Whitman himself would have understood:

How shall we praise the magnificence of the dead,
The great man humbled, the haughty brought to dust?
Is there a horn we should not blow as proudly
For the meanest of us all, who creeps his days,
Guarding his heart from blows, to die obscurely?
I am no king, have laid no kingdoms waste,
Taken no princes captive, led no triumphs
Of weeping women through long walls of trumpets . . .

Close to forty years later the humanism and the relativism were still there, finding a sparer and pithier form in Part IX of the title poem of *A Letter from Li Po* (1955):

The winds of doctrine blow both ways at once.
The wetted finger feels the wind each way,
presaging plums from north, and snow from south.
The dust-wind whistles from the eastern sea
to dry the nectarine and parch the mouth.
The west wind from the desert wreathes the rain

too late to fill our wells, but soon enough,
the four-day rain that bears the leaves away. •
Song with the wind will change, but is still song
and pierces to the rightness in the wrong
or makes the wrong a rightness, a delight.
Where are the eager guests that yesterday
thronged at the gate? Like leaves, they could not stay,
the winds of doctrine blew their minds away,
and we shall have no loving-cup tonight.
No loving-cup: for not ourselves are here
to entertain us in that outer year,
where, so they say, we see the Greater Earth.
The winds of doctrine blow our minds away,
and we are absent till another birth.

There can be little doubt that Aiken's independence of the neoclassicism brought in by such men as Hulme and Eliot and his equal independence of the automatic Marxisms of the 1930's were costly to his vogue. Nor did the New Criticism find his work congenial to explication, an activity that could have made it more well known than it has been to university students of recent decades. One result, quite apart from the matter of his fame in general, is that much remains to be understood about the interaction of Aiken and his time. It is not merely that he has still to receive due credit for the concerned, cosmopolitan, and equable attitudes he displayed toward the nightmare issues and events of social politics in the last fifty years. It is also that his art, with its manifold sources in American rebellion and European sophistication, is worthy of even fuller exploration than it has received.

The anonymous writer of the lead article in the London *Times Literary Supplement* of April 19, 1963, credited Aiken with being original in advance of his time and the possessor of a cosmic sense that outsoars Eliot and Pound. The writer continued: ". . . increasingly poetry has become a way of writing, not a way of thinking. Yet not to like Aiken (or Shelley, of course) is a confession of not being capable of thinking in poetic terms; that is to say with the whole consciousness."

Aiken has created a fluent and colorful picturization of man learning to enjoy and realize himself. The process is conceived of as a response to a universal challenge, first in the sense that the ancestral gods are against enjoyment and ultimately in the sense that enjoyment leads to a need to transcend itself. The poetic art in which he embodies this view of life is Indian in its luxuriance, repetition, and decoration. It stands over against the sparer poetic line that has won much of the lip service as well as some of the practice of the more influential poets since Hulme and Pound made their voices felt half a century ago. The energetic profusion of Aiken has a masculine bouquet that allies him more closely with Yeats and Tate than with most of his contemporaries. Aiken, as they say, has written lines below his own best level and was thoughtful enough in his *Selected Poems* of 1961 to anthologize himself at his best. His lifelong performance in a luxuriant style is not only one of the strongest testaments to the power of his youthful insights but also the preserver of a tradition whose vitality, we should be glad to say, he has helped to pass on.

↲ Selected Bibliography

Works of Conrad Aiken

POETRY

Earth Triumphant and Other Tales in Verse. New York: Macmillan, 1914.

Turns and Movies and Other Tales in Verse. Boston: Houghton Mifflin; London: Constable, 1916.

The Jig of Forslin: A Symphony. Boston: Four Seas, 1916; London: Secker, 1921.

Nocturne of Remembered Spring and Other Poems. London: Secker, 1916; Boston: Four Seas, 1917.

The Charnel Rose; Senlin: A Biography; and Other Poems. Boston: Four Seas, 1918.

The House of Dust: A Symphony. Boston: Four Seas, 1920.

Punch: The Immortal Liar, Documents in His History. New York: Knopf; London: Secker, 1921.

Priapus and the Pool. Cambridge, Mass.: Dunster House, Harvard University, 1922.

The Pilgrimage of Festus. New York: Knopf, 1923; London: Secker, 1924.

Priapus and the Pool and Other Poems. New York: Boni and Liveright, 1925.

Prelude. New York: Random House, 1929.

Selected Poems. New York: Scribner's, 1929.

John Deth: A Metaphysical Legend, and Other Poems. New York: Scribner's, 1930.

The Coming Forth by Day of Osiris Jones. New York: Scribner's, 1931.

Preludes for Memnon. New York: Scribner's, 1931.

And in the Hanging Gardens. Baltimore: Garamond, 1933.

Landscape West of Eden. London: Dent, 1934; New York: Scribner's, 1935.

Time in the Rock; Preludes to Definition. New York: Scribner's, 1936.

And in the Human Heart. New York: Duell, Sloan, and Pearce, 1940.

Brownstone Eclogues and Other Poems. New York: Duell, Sloan, and Pearce, 1942.

The Soldier: A Poem. Norfolk, Conn.: New Directions, 1944.

The Kid. New York: Duell, Sloan, and Pearce, 1947.

Skylight One: Fifteen Poems. New York: Oxford University Press, 1949.

The Divine Pilgrim. Athens: University of Georgia Press, 1949.

Collected Poems. New York: Oxford University Press, 1953.
A Letter from Li Po and Other Poems. New York: Oxford University Press, 1955.
Sheepfold Hill: Fifteen Poems. New York: Sagamore Press, 1958.
Selected Poems. New York: Oxford University Press, 1961.
The Morning Song of Lord Zero. New York: Oxford University Press, 1963.

NOVELS

Blue Voyage. New York: Scribner's; London: Howe, 1927.
Great Circle. New York: Scribner's; London: Wishart, 1933.
King Coffin. New York: Scribner's; London: Dent, 1935.
A Heart for the Gods of Mexico. London: Secker, 1939.
Conversation: or, Pilgrim's Progress. New York: Duell, Sloan, and Pearce, 1940.

SHORT STORIES

Bring! Bring! and Other Stories. New York: Boni and Liveright; London: Secker, 1925.
Costumes by Eros. New York: Scribner's, 1928; London: Cape, 1929.
Among the Lost People. New York: Scribner's, 1934.
The Short Stories of Conrad Aiken. New York: Duell, Sloan, and Pearce, 1950.
Collected Short Stories. Cleveland, Ohio: World, 1960.

PLAY

Mr. Arcularis. Cambridge, Mass.: Harvard University Press, 1957.

CRITICISM AND OTHER PROSE

Scepticisms: Notes on Contemporary Poetry. New York: Knopf, 1919.
Foreword to *Two Wessex Tales* by Thomas Hardy. Boston: Four Seas Company, 1919.
Introduction to *Selected Poems of Emily Dickinson*. London: Cape, 1924.
Ushant: An Essay. New York and Boston: Duell, Sloan, and Pearce–Little, Brown, 1952.
A Reviewer's ABC: Collected Criticism, edited by Rufus A. Blanshard. New York: Meridian, 1958.

CURRENT AMERICAN REPRINTS

Brownstone Eclogues. Bloomington: Midland (Indiana University Press). $1.75.
Ushant. Cleveland, Ohio: Meridian (World). $1.75.

Bibliographies

Cheney, Frances. *Sixty American Poets 1896–1944: A Preliminary Check-List*, selected with Preface and Critical Notes by Allen Tate. Washington, D.C.: Library of Congress, 1945. Pp. 3–6.

Stallman, R. W. "Annotated Checklist on Conrad Aiken: A Critical Study," in *Wake 11*, edited by Seymour Lawrence. New York: Wake Editions, 1952. Pp. 114–21.

Critical Studies

Hoffman, Frederick J. *Conrad Aiken*. New York: Twayne, 1962.

Lawrence, Seymour, ed. Conrad Aiken Number, *Wake 11*. New York: Wake Editions, 1952.

Martin, Jay. *Conrad Aiken, A Life of His Art*. Princeton, N.J.: Princeton University Press, 1962.

Peterson, Houston. *The Melody of Chaos*. New York and Toronto: Longmans, Green, 1931.

Articles and Reviews

"Answer to the Sphinx," *Times Literary Supplement* (London), April 19, 1963, pp. 257–58.

Beach, Joseph Warren. "Conrad Aiken and T. S. Eliot: Echoes and Overtones," *PMLA*, 69:753–62 (1954).

Benedetti, Anna. "Sinfonie in Versi," *Nuova Antologia*, 204:202–6 (January 16, 1920).

Blackmur, Richard P. "Mr. Aiken's Second Wind," *New Republic*, 89:335 (January 13, 1937).

Kunitz, Stanley. "The Poetry of Conrad Aiken," *Nation*, 133:393–94 (October 14, 1931).

Moore, Marianne. "If a Man Die," *Hound and Horn*, 5:313–20 (January–March 1932).

Schwarz, Delmore. "Merry Go Round of Opinion," *New Republic*, 108:292–93 (March 1, 1943).

Tate, Allen. "The Author of *John Deth*," *New Republic*, 68:265–66 (July 22, 1931).

———. "Conrad Aiken's Poetry," *Nation*, 122:38–39 (January 13, 1926).

Van Doren, Mark. "Effects in Verse," *Nation*, 112:86–87 (January 19, 1921).

Winters, Yvor. Review of *Selected Poems* in *Hound and Horn*, 3:454–61 (April–June 1930).